For Emma

— C.N.

Copyright © 2002 by Nancy Hall, Inc.
All rights reserved. Published by Scholastic Inc.
Printed in the U.S.A.

ISBN 0-439-57143-X

4 5 6 7 8 9 10   23   12 11 10 09 08 07 06 05 04

Harriet Tubman

by Catherine Nichols
Illustrated by Brian Denington

SCHOLASTIC INC.
New York Toronto London Auckland Sydney
Mexico City New Delhi Hong Kong Buenos Aires

Harriet Tubman was born
on a Maryland plantation in the South.
The year was probably 1820,
but no one knows for sure.
That's because Harriet was born a slave.
A slave's date of birth was not
written down.

No one knew that Harriet would grow up
to be a brave woman.
No one knew that someday she would
lead hundreds of people to freedom.

As a child, Harriet had a nickname—
Minty.
When Minty was around six years old,
she was put to work.
Her job was to wind yarn into balls.
If the yarn broke, she was whipped.

Later, Minty was given a new job.
She checked muskrat traps.
Minty had to walk barefoot
in cold rivers.
Still, she liked this work better than
winding yarn.

One day, Minty woke up sick.
When she was better, she was not allowed
in the river anymore.
It was back to winding yarn for Minty.

When Minty was older,
she worked in the fields.

One day, she saw a slave
try to escape.
The slave ran into a store.
The field boss followed him.
So did Minty.

Then the slave ran out of the store.
This time Minty stood in the doorway.
She refused to move.
The boss picked up a heavy weight.
He threw it at the slave.
He missed.
The weight hit Minty instead.

Minty was badly hurt.
When she got better, she had a long scar
on her forehead.
She would sometimes fall asleep suddenly.

The other slaves were proud of Minty.
She had stood up to the boss.
They no longer called her Minty.
She was Harriet now.

In 1844, Harriet married John Tubman.
John was a free man.
No one owned him.
Yet Harriet was still a slave.

One day, Harriet learned that
she was going to be sold.
She would have to leave her family.
Harriet told John that she wanted
to escape.
She wanted him to go with her.
John didn't want to go.
He also didn't want Harriet to escape.
He told her that if she tried,
he would tell her master!

Harriet waited for John to fall asleep.
Then she packed some food
and left the cabin.

Harriet knew that some people
wanted to help slaves.
These people ran a special railroad—
the *Underground Railroad.*
This railroad didn't have trains.
It was made up of people who hid slaves
and helped them escape.
The slaves were called *passengers.*

Harriet knew where one such
woman lived.
The woman helped Harriet.
She told Harriet how to get
to the next safe house.

Harriet traveled only at night.
During the day people would be
looking for her.

Harriet walked quickly through
the dark woods.
She followed the North Star.
She knew it would lead her
to the North—to freedom.

After several days, Harriet crossed over
to Pennsylvania, a free state in the North.
Free states didn't allow slavery.
Harriet had dreamed of this moment
for a long time.
Now it had finally happened.
She was free!

Harriet found work in a hotel.
But she didn't forget her family.
She wanted them to be free, too.

One day she learned that her sister's family
was about to be sold.
Harriet went back to the South
and helped them escape.

Harriet continued helping slaves escape.
Each time the danger grew.
Slave owners had found out about Harriet.
They offered a reward for her.
They wanted her caught—dead or alive!

But Harriet didn't stop.
Sometimes she disguised herself.
She would dress as a man
or as an old woman.

One day Harriet went back
for her husband.
John met her at the cabin door.
He told her he did not want to leave
his home.
Sadly, Harriet walked away.
She never saw John again.

Harriet helped many people escape.
But her parents were still slaves.
They were old now.
Traveling on foot would be hard for them.
Harriet wanted her parents to be
free though.

In 1857, she went back for them.
She made a simple wagon
and hitched a horse to it.
Then she drove her parents
away from slavery!

In 1861, war broke out.
The states in the North wanted
to free the slaves.
The states in the South did not.

Harriet helped the North.
She worked as a nurse.
She cared for sick soldiers.

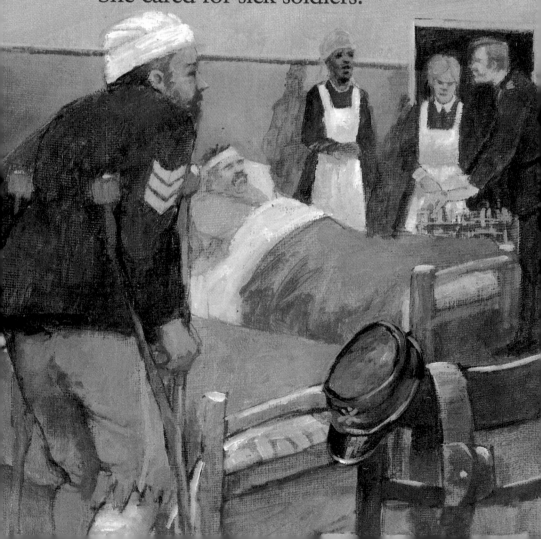

In 1865, the war ended.
The North had won.
Now all slaves were free!

Harriet continued to help people.
She returned to her home
in Auburn, New York.
There, she cared for her parents.
She also cared for former slaves.
Harriet never turned anyone away.

In 1913, Harriet Tubman died.
The people of Auburn honored her.
Flags were flown at half-mast.
Famous people spoke.
Everyone agreed that Harriet Tubman
had been a brave woman.

In her lifetime, Harriet Tubman helped
more than 300 slaves escape.
She never lost a passenger
on the Underground Railroad.
And she was never caught!